I0569595

Refined

Refined

Kezia Kyei-Boahen

Copyright © 2024 by Kezia Kyei-Boahen
All rights reserved. No part of this publication may be reproduced, stored or transmitted in any form or by any means, electronic, mechanical, photocopying, recording, scanning, or otherwise without written permission from the publisher. It is illegal to copy this book, post it to a website, or distribute it by any other means without permission. For information, contact the publisher at kezkyei@gmail.com.

First edition

Scripture quotations marked (CEV) are from the Contemporary English Version Copyright © 1991, 1992, 1995 by American Bible Society. Used by Permission.

Scriptures taken from the Holy Bible, New International Version®, NIV®. Copyright © 1973, 1978, 1984, 2011 by Biblica, Inc.™ Used by permission of Zondervan. All rights reserved worldwide. www.zondervan.com The "NIV" and "New International Version" are trademarks registered in the United States Patent and Trademark Office by Biblica, Inc.™

Book cover was designed by Liana Torres.

Dedication

To **Jesus, My Mom, Barbara; Lili Skinner,**
and those who can and can't relate

1 Peter 1:7 CEV

"Your faith will be like gold that has been tested in a fire. And these trials will prove that your faith is worth much more than gold that can be destroyed. They will show that you will be given praise and honor and glory when Jesus Christ returns."

Contents

Part One

Trigger Point

Standing across from the Tempter and myself,
Trying to regain consciousness of who I am.
When he tried to fire a bullet into my heart,
I used God's Word to protect myself from it.

I'm wandering into the alleyway
of what remained that day.
I've gotten better ever since,
But there's still a pulsing pain
within the reminiscence,
That's driving me insane.

I used to think that indulging in my dirty thoughts
wouldn't make me fall apart,
But it slowly did—
No wonder why death makes up the wages of sin.

But let's get back to this scene and figure out what's
making my heart bleed,
Where from this puddle of blood—
WAIT A MINUTE, I'VE BEEN SHOT!

I see the bullet that penetrated my heart
Lying on the ground, completely still—
While my heart screams from the agonizing jolts,
Hindering its weak beating pattern,
Emphasizing how difficult it is to breathe.
I feel dizzy,
Running out of oxygen that tries to cling to my veins,
Panicking, wondering where to begin;
Hoping it's not my death day.

I must retreat before the Enemy makes a bloodbath out
of me,
But the pain becomes overwhelming
and takes over all that I see.
I close my eyes in agony.
As blood oozes to the ground,
Covering up the whole crime scene.
I weep on my knees,
And the only thing that's coming back is the
memories—

The Enemy laughed in my face after I fell into his trap,
but I stayed,
While he shot me once again:

With the lies that I remain depressed,

With the lies that I declare myself a mess,

With the lies that my sins don't matter,

With the lies that tell me I'm alone—

But all that did was make me shatter.

Except this time, I start to fight back and wrap up my wounds,

Get back on my firm foundation—the Truth.

But the Enemy sees this as a threat and works even harder to get into my head.

Thankful that my persistence hasn't let me down,

Because there's a war happening in this sacred town.

However, the Enemy began to wind down,

then proceeded to walk away with scars on his face.

After I fought and dodged his next round of bullets to form blood clots in my faith,

Blocking my arteries from receiving the oxygen-rich blood I need.

I figured I had won until he returned with a particular gaze—

One that was oddly familiar, like he was unsatisfied.

He cocks his gun one last time.

And says, "You would've won if you had God by your side."

I wonder, "Where was God this whole time?"

Truth is, He never left me.

But that's something the Devil doesn't want me to believe,

So he gaslights me

Into believing that his lies are true—

That these roots aren't new,

That my past isn't outgrown,

Rather evident in the battle.

To add to this bloodshed,

He shoots me, "Especially when you have depression."

You see, the Enemy just pulled a trigger
To get you to consider the possibility
That your present isn't your reality,
Since you look the same but have grown tremendously.

This trigger point isn't something minor
But rather major, as it will grab your attention
And make you rethink and question
Every step you've taken.

But you have a choice to make.

Let the bullet enter your heart, make space, and penetrate,

For the lies to sprout and grow as they topple the roots that once glowed,

Or rely on what God has done in your life and use His Word to refute the "truth" the Devil wants to speak in you.

Choose wisely, for the choice you make will determine your next step in life.

Just know that your trigger point may still be in the card deck,

even if you refuse to fall for his lies.

The important part is remembering that you're a new creation

and acknowledging the weaknesses of your previous seasons.

Let's go back to the beginning.

Made New

The Mask

I had an attitude that was invisible—it wasn't something that I claimed to show.

People suggested I was sad, but honestly, I was depressed and easily got upset by their comparison,

As if there were no difference between these two words that were often used interchangeably.

This made me even more enraged because those words hold two distinct and different meanings.

To me, I felt like I couldn't be myself and had to hide my true state because constantly,

The only thing people saw was the depression in me.

Then, in the instances when despair blossomed as I drifted into my thoughts,

I would get scolded to discontinue this practice—but told to resume the practice of being someone I was not.

I did as I was told.

I felt lost as I painted on this fake smile everywhere I went,

But people had the wrong interpretations.

Just because the leaves are alive doesn't mean the roots are too.

Just because you see a person smiling doesn't mean they aren't drowning.

Therefore, I became complacent about keeping my sunny side up.

But my chin was down, as I was becoming more corrupt—

The darkness was too much,

To the point where I wanted to give up.

This was the season that I hoped would fade away,

Like the clouds reappearing after a rainy day.

Thankfully, God saved me.

So, I urge you to not lose hope,

And to put the facade away.

Testimony

It was one summer night in 2020,

Where I lay in bed, ignoring that I'm hungry.

Scrolling on TikTok until my Wi-Fi broke.

Once it did, I sat there and sulked.

Because the depression inside me wasn't dying,

Instead, it was surprisingly inclining,

Since I kept my smile painted on my mask,

With vibrant colors to hide my vulnerability, which was the task.

However, keeping this facade wasn't easy anymore,

Since I became immune to knowing what's real behind these doors.

But distractions made things easier,

Except for the fact that I felt trapped—

Like walls closing in,

Or perhaps cracks within my mask,

That would expose my past of what I used to do and watch.

Oh man, let me just stop—

I had to keep the facade

That everything was okay,

That I was the perfect Christian child, with straight A's.

Unfortunately, it led me to hate myself—

even one day, I heard a voice telling me to make that choice:

"end it all and not be afraid, since no one would love you,"

But thankfully, I was not persuaded.

But that didn't stop the negativity—

All the 'guys would never like you' and

the 'you wish you were me.'

All these voices telling me I'll never succeed,

and that there is no light at the end of the tunnel for me.

But thankfully, I went back to TikTok that night

and scrolled upon a video that would change the course of my life.

It was this person who urged me to pray and give my life to God.

I figured I couldn't hold onto these thoughts,

So, I gave it a shot.

The best decision I ever made in my life—

Because of His sacrifice,

I was now set free from the cinderblock that was chained to my feet,

That once drowned me in the darkness of defeat.

Kezia Kyei-Boahen

What is Home?

What is home?

A place where I can be myself—

Where condemnation is replaced with conviction.

No tears, no weeping, no worries,

Just rejoicing in what God is doing in my life.

Although in the valley, it feels rough,

I rejoice, knowing what God has done and will do—

Is home.

Lukewarm

Here's the thing—

You did care when others didn't,

You even gave Your life for me.

I wonder how it was

When I wasn't living in harmony with the person You wanted me to be.

How my misunderstanding of lukewarmness and complacency affected those who truly wanted to live as Christians.

How my flawed definition of Christian—

Still living in this world and having so much to do with sin—

Affected those who wanted to listen to Your Word and change from within.

Remembering who I used to be, I'm glad I'm a new creation,

A Christian who encourages Light from within,

While also fighting the leeches of sin.

I'm sorry for those I've influenced, leading them back to the darkness I once saw as the only light.

May they experience what it means to be changed by Your sacrifice in their lives.

Please forgive the iniquities of my past,

And I thank You for being with me, especially on days I thought would be my last.

"The iniquities of your past have been forgiven.

You are now a new Creation.

You are in Me, your new life has begun.

Therefore, sin no more, my child, whom I love."

—God

Unworthy

Unworthy of His love,
Unworthy of His grace,
Unworthy of Him taking my place.

The cross is where I am free.
This is who I should be:
The unashamed one—like He.
The cross is where I have hope,
The cross is where I cope.

Because I know that He is the one who brings the true
light inside of me.

As I feel darkened by this world
And the sinful desires,
The temptations that come at me
Can inspire

The hope that is not hope,
And the trust that is not trust,
That just betrays me over and over.
And I just must

Avoid them.

I know they can be hard to overcome,

But with His strength—

I can do all things

Through Him

Who strengthens me.

I know I'm not alone

In this place some call home.

I will have hope and faith till the day He comes back,

And remind myself of His grace.

Unworthy of His love,

Unworthy of His grace,

I'm unworthy of Him taking my place

Bold Faith

I love being bold in my faith,

Showing how His grace changes me,

And talking about what Jesus did on the cross to save me.

I am not ashamed of the Gospel,

For it brings salvation to those who believe.

Therefore, we should spread the Good News and see what it

brings

To those who are unforgiven, in chains, and unfree;

To become like those who have been restored and redeemed.

If I get made fun of, I don't care.

Instead, I'm glad I planted the seed,

Knowing what Jesus on the cross means to me.

I encourage you to be bold in faith,

Talk with Jesus and praise His Name,

Share the Gospel when given the opportunity.

Stay rooted in Jesus,

Keep planting seeds,

Don't worry about the outcome,

And be with the Holy Spirit in unity.

The Shifting Tide

Can I be Real?

Sometimes, it gets negative,

And I don't know what to do.

At those times, I feel farthest from the Truth.

In one ear, I hear the Devil's lies,

Creating insecurities and reminding me of embarrassing moments,

Trying to get me to the point where I don't confide in Christ.

It gets hard sometimes,

Thinking about everyone else's lives and comparing theirs to mine.

It seems so blissful, and at times,

I feel like the only one with these lies

Invading my thoughts, making me question

How God created me.

I go to school, and I just want to come home—

To my room, all alone, and cry openly like a waterfall,

talking to God about my problems and letting them go.

Honestly, I think some people just don't know

What goes through my mind,

The number of questions and lies that flow.

But there are those times too,

When I feel confident in faith—

Letting that cleanse me as I go through the day.

And I love it. I love being bold in my faith.

It's the highlight of my day,

Knowing that I'm an ambassador of Christ and perhaps someone gets saved

By what God has done and is doing in me—even to this day.

I remember this morning,

I was so excited because my friend, whom I've been praying for,

Wanted to recommit her life to Christ, which encouraged me.

Bro, God is so good.

And even when my moments aren't as blissful and peaceful,

I can remember what God is doing in other people's lives,

Knowing that He is still at work

Growing Plant

I'm just trying to stay focused,
Trusting God and His speech.
I've been fighting my hardest
In this storm, not to conform.

Even when it isn't reflected,
Sometimes it's hard to understand
What I'm truly going through
And hoping it lines up with His plan.

Trying to keep fighting
While running the race,
Remembering it's okay
To go at a different pace.

Often, I feel like I'm a sitting duck,
Watching the waves crash,
Except I'm stuck.

Don't know where I am now—
Lukewarm or being spit out,

Trying to find my way somehow,
Yet the current is pulling me away now.

Can't tell why my passion is decreasing,
And the days feel like they're breezing,
Other than the fact that we're in the end times,
And I'm not ready, and it gets scary.

Why am I wasting time on these earthly things
While my faith isn't what I've planned for it to be?

Why can't I find satisfaction in what I've been blessed
with,
When I'm stuck in the trials, trying to learn lessons?

Why is my stamina "too low to fight"
When God gave me the oxygen I need?

Summer was supposed to be the season where I got to
spend so much time with God,
Or so I assumed, for it has led to a bunch of trials and a
hurricane of thoughts.

I'm going to be truthful,
I wasn't expecting summer to be like this, but it's a
blessing.
My faith is being tested

And has a chance to grow with endurance—
God's plan was to make my faith stronger.
How come I didn't know it?

Well, that's amazing.
God is giving me the opportunity to grow,
Like a plant being taken care of after being in the snow,
With scabbed branches and crooked leaves.

Then given the chance
To grow and breathe
As a new plant.

Therefore, I now understand that my faith is like a plant—

It has opportunities to grow.
It needs time.
It needs checking up on and improvement.
It should be fed, not starved.
Okay, I don't know why this sounds like a pet, but anyway—
It needs more than just the minimum.
And it can't make it on its own.

It's okay to ask for help.

It's okay to have different atmospheres or temperatures.
But the fact that it perseveres through the struggle
Helps it grow like a new person.

These trials will come and go,
But your faith, through them, can grow.

Don't be discouraged when you're in trials that are
neck-deep.
Keep your head high and think
About what this means
And how to seek God through it all.
For me, it's through poetry.

Stressed & Burnout

Schoolwork piles up,

My mind is clogged with many thoughts—

Assignments that are due, emotions, and upcoming tests

Make me question—what's next?

What happens when I can't rest? Can't I get a break?

I want to get away

From my feelings and thoughts and stay

In a place where I feel complacent,

In this place, in this journey,

And what I left on the road, as well as the amazing scenery.

I'm not having a good day

Regarding my sentiments,

Since I don't know what to think.

School is becoming intensely stressful each week,

Not enough self-care time

To give a break to my mind.

This is already hard for me,

Because I have so much to do.

Not enough rest, not enough time to refresh,

And decide what to do next,

Without burnout flooding my steps.

Numb

You ever had the feeling where you feel alone?
You ever had the feeling that you didn't know where to go?
The feeling that feels numb
As it sits at the top of your tongue.

You think about it often,
Trying to understand something
About what it is,
About how it is—
There, I don't know how I feel right now.
I don't know what to think about—

My relationship with God?
I can't say it's the best right now.

But I'm trying to rest
From school and everything else
That may develop stress.
But life becomes bittersweet.

Especially with the wars that might be happening,

I've been praying for those people in those countries.
I pray for their protection and safety.

I often feel like I'm not always fulfilling my
expectations,
Which leads to me feeling unmotivated and devastated.

Reflecting on my day,
I barely talked to God all day.
I don't really know what to say.

I know in Luke 18:1,
It says we shouldn't stop praying.
But here I am, falling short
AGAIN

Motion Sickness

Hello, hello,
I know I'm not in
The usual routine
In the time I spend with You.

I know, I know,
I'm supposed to be faithful,
I'm supposed to pray more
And stay true.

But it gets hard.
I give in to temptations,
Leading to devastation
From expectations far from the truth

Of what I
Wanted reality to be:
Me not giving in
To the temptations I see.

And the fact

That I've failed again,
And You lift me up
With Your right hand,

And how You never
Gave up on me,
Just makes me see
Your love, and

It makes me
Feel emotional
Just to be told
You love me.

From multiple perspectives
And multiple people—
Your message,
Their sequel.

I'm sorry,
I sin excessively, and I don't know how to stop.

I'm sorry
That my faith isn't invincible

I'm sorry

For my flawed representation of how Christians are
supposed to be.

I'm sorry
For not relying on Your Word.

I'm sorry.
I've failed once again.
—Kezia.

"Kezia,
Don't drown yourself in pity.
I accept your apology.
I know it's hard to fight back,
But remember you have community—

People you can go to for advice, prayer, and guidance,
As well as to be encouraged.

Never think that I don't love you!
There is a reason why it's been repeated numerous times.
It's not a lie, and it remains despite what you do.

Yes, you sin and fall short,
But remember, I died for you.

And I love you.

There's grace, that is available to you—

And the guilt, regret, and your action of making this prayer

Will and can guide you to repentance and knowing the truth:

"Love wins."

And I will always love you!"

—God

Time

I'm not ready.
I'm not at the place I want to be
In my relationship with God
Because it's not how it seems.

Everything is not going blissfully and peacefully;
Instead, it's draining me—

The outside factors that take away my time
From the One who is really Divine.

School, self-care, and everything else that's assigned—

Let me ask you:
How much more will you take of my time?
How much more will you drain me in despise?
Stress over grades and not enough leisure time—
How much more will it continue to rise?

It's interesting because in summer I wanted to be in
school,

Sharing my faith around the halls, dodging Satan's bullets too,

Yet it gets tiring being in an environment that bombards you with "to-dos,"

Not enough time to pray and snooze.

I mean, yes, the harvest is plenty,

But is it worth being invasive to many

And not having the strength to run to God with burdens too heavy to carry?

Since when did school take away the time for my independence?

The time to have fun and enjoy my weekends—

The time to spend with God in my regions.

Time is not going to wait for me, as my mom says,

But when it ends and eternity comes, will I be ready?

I guess I'll just reside my thoughts here and see

What God may tell me through poetry.

Under The Surface

I Don't Know

Here I am,
Getting tempted again.
Don't know if it's just in my head,
Or if it's the truth instead.
I don't know what to think—
Like it's either me or the Enemy,
Or God speaking, but I don't know much,
Because I keep taking shots,
And it's getting harder to get back up.

Why is it the same things I'm getting tempted about?
The realness of friendships,
Relationship status,
What other people think of me,
And that I'm alone.

Wake up, go to school, and don't want to be there.
Feel myself plastering my fake smile like I did before—
I thought I wasn't going back to this lifestyle.
I thought I was done—
Done being fake with myself.

I don't know what happened.

I don't know how to be a positive influence on people.

I don't know how to balance life and my relationship
with God,

And the temptations and fake thoughts.

"I feel like giving up."

I've had these thoughts every two days,

Especially as I feel like everyone's second choice,

Even to myself. But honestly,

It's all because of me overthinking,

And now, I think I'm losing who I am.

I don't know

What to do,

What to say,

What to think.

What's real?

What's not?

I don't know.

Counterfeit

Why does it feel counterfeit?

My salvation, my calling, my passion—

My prayers, my cries, my Christ-like behavior,

Everything being okay, forgiving and loving everyone,

Not being the dog that returns to her vomit—

Why does it feel so counterfeit?

Like, what's the point anymore?

What's the point of repenting, then getting back up and digging yourself into a deeper hole?

Chokehold

Questioning everything,
As if I'm dreaming,
I'm in this coma
That's far from utopia.

Living in my regrets,
Which replay in my head,
Telling me to do this or
Do that instead.

But the past is the past,
Including this civil war,
Telling me I've lost
What I've been fighting for.

I would tell myself
Not to throw in the towel,
But, bro, what's the point
When I've been in this chokehold for hours?

Choked by death,

By my flesh,

That drowns me

With the sand—

The sand that became my comfort

When I lost my stand,

But now I'm in quicksand,

Sinking in bland faith.

Backsliding

I ponder these thoughts that hold no weight.
I have a question, one that can't wait—
What do you do when you're backsliding?
What do you do when you decide to give up?
When you decide you can't do it anymore?

"The facade must come down.
You must seek help.
You must not go through this alone,"
You may say.
Well, it's easier said than done.

Civil War

Fighting my flesh,
Wishing it would end—
The same fight,
The same concept.

Civil war—
Not really much from the outside,
But inside, it's a whole war.
I keep it closed in,
Hoping nobody reports this domestic violence.

What's the point?
Why should I fight?
Why do I struggle with fighting for what's right—
My salvation?
Yet, I don't know if it's worth fighting for.

My soldiers are coming back,
Reporting that this war has to end.
The number of deaths outnumber sin.

Pleading for me to make a compromise with the Enemy,

But, Lord knows, I would never commit such an
atrocity.

Now my armed soldiers wait,

But time is counting down.

I have to make a decision,

And I have to do it now.

Tell the soldiers to get on the defensive line

And start to pray,

Like Moses did

On those days.

Where he prayed

And offered sacrifices to God

While there was an army

That came from afar.

But once he prayed,

God set the Enemy back.

As they continued to triumph,

And thanked God for having their backs.

So, I urge you,

Have the same faith

In the Civil War,

In the pain,

In the triumphs,

And the rain.

Because we know who will really win this war,

And we know that the enemy will

Never soar,

Nor will the enemy win

In this raging war.

Figuring it Out

I'm trying not to give up
In this walk—
Man, it's been rough.

Questioning my salvation,
'Cause I'm getting tempted
By the same sin
I've struggled with
A bunch of times.

If I'm being honest—
What happened to being saved?

I don't know what I'm going through at this moment.
My wounds are no longer covered by a bandage.

I'm trying not to comply
With my past self.
Man, I'm trying hard to ignore
All these past thoughts that tell me
I'm inadequate and shouldn't be here.

But at the same time,
I preach that 'everything is alright,'
But it's the opposite
Since I'm indulging in the same sins.

So, if I'm being honest,
I don't know what's happening.

I'm in this storm,
Except it's my faith that is withering.

I want to give up.
Not sure what my purpose is,
'Cause every time I move,
I get stuck in cement.

Walking everywhere
With a smile drawn on my face,
Telling everyone 'this girl's different,'
But at times, I don't feel saved.

And I'll be honest, for at least this moment—
What happened to being saved?

Why is it that one day I'm enjoying the sunset,
And the next day I'm drowning in the rain?

Kezia Kyei-Boahen

On the Fence

I'm on the fence,
Swayed by my emotions to
Move toward the flesh or
Stay true to my intentions
And fight the darkness.

Nevertheless, I don't know where I am.
I'm just distant.
Am I moving forward?
Am I moving backward?

Spiral Street

I'm getting tired. I'm walking down
A road I thought I'd well passed by now.
Going through some cycles,
Not knowing where
My destination is—and I'm not going to swear.

But I know, I feel something different.
I know I need to keep listening.
I know that I am a new creation, but why do I feel the
same in this location?

I'm kneeling down, crying now.
I don't know where I am; I'm trying to figure that out.
Why am I lost?
What happened to
Following Him—
The One and Only Truth?

Oh, my faith is in ruins,
But why am I in this space?
Where its growth was just the same,

And condemnation keeps calling out my name!

"So tell me when
You're going to let Me in.
You're crying,
And you need someone to lean on—
Someone to
Know what you're going through,
Someone who would
Understand you.

And please don't go.
Don't give up,
Since you have passion and perseverance.
You know what you've got to do.
And I'm telling you, please continue walking with the
Truth!

And I will always be here for you.
I still love you and adore you,
Even more, as I died on the cross,
So, Kezia, please come home.

You are already forgiven,
My child.

Come abide in grace.

Come abide in My Name."

—God

Rest Stop

On a road trip, but not a fun one,
Questioning my faith, like it's a ransom.
Should I preserve it or let it die?
I don't know, so I soar
To the point where my head is in the sky,
Running on autopilot like it's my gas line.

Don't really know if I'll come back
To the light, the true treasure on this map.
Since this fight has been hell for me—
I know, wow, "cursing in poetry."
But if that word doesn't describe it,
I don't know what will.

Almost went back to thoughts as if I were writing my
will,
Dead but still alive? Should I continue the fight?

'Cause at this point, I'm tired, and I'm going under
anesthesia,
Giving up on God because I thought He let me down.

Thought I would be healed considering how well known I am in this town.

In this town, which is where home is—

But I feel so invasive, insecure because of my uncertainty.

Maybe I should just leave.

"Who would care?"

"Who would even know?"

Thoughts like these are the ones that flow.

At this point, I'm not sure I'm even in control,

Considering where I am isn't where I grow.

Or am I growing? I don't know.

This spiritual warfare has cut up my hope,

Leaving me in my past, where my depression grew.

Thought that fruit was burned when I was reborn into the truth.

But truth is, I'm not sure anymore.

Could I consider that I will struggle evermore?

That God didn't just take away the pain, but wanted to heal me from it.

Is that why this spiritual warfare has been so consistent?

Welcome Back

(let's resume from where we started)

Trigger Point

Standing across from the Tempter and myself,
Trying to regain consciousness of who I am.
When he tried to fire a bullet into my heart,
I used God's Word to protect myself from it.

I'm wandering into the alleyway
Of what remained that day.
I've gotten better ever since,
But there's still a pulsing pain
Within the reminisce,
That's driving me insane.

I used to think that indulging in my dirty thoughts
Wouldn't make me fall apart,
But it slowly did—
No wonder why death makes up the wages of sin.

But let's get back to this scene
And figure out what's making my heart bleed,
Where from this puddle of blood—

WAIT A MINUTE, I'VE BEEN SHOT!

I see the bullet that penetrated my heart

Lying on the ground, completely still—

While my heart screams from the agonizing jolts,

Hindering its weak beating pattern,

Emphasizing how difficult it is to breathe.

I feel dizzy,

Running out of oxygen that tries to cling to my veins,

Panicking, wondering where to begin,

Hoping it's not my death day.

I must retreat before the Enemy makes a bloodbath out of me,

But the pain becomes overwhelming

And takes over all that I see.

I close my eyes in agony.

As blood oozes to the ground, covering up the whole crime scene.

I weep on my knees,

And the only thing that's coming back is the memories—

The Enemy laughed in my face after I fell into his trap, but I stayed

While he shot me once again:

With the lies that I remain depressed,

With the lies that declare me a mess,

With the lies that my sins don't matter,

With the lies that tell me I'm alone—

But all that did was make me shatter.

Except this time, I start to fight back and wrap up my wounds,

Get back on my firm foundation—the Truth.

But the enemy sees this as a threat and works even harder to get into my head.

Thankful that my persistence hasn't let me down,

Because there's a war happening in this sacred town.

However, the Enemy began to wind down,

Then proceeded to walk away with scars on his face.

After I fought and dodged his next round of bullets to form blood clots in my faith,

Blocking my arteries from receiving the oxygen-rich blood I need.

I figured I had won until he returned with a particular gaze—

One that was oddly familiar, like he was unsatisfied.

He cocks his gun one last time.

And says, "You would've won if you had God by your side."

I wonder, "Where was God this whole time?"

Truth is, He never left me.

But that's something the Devil doesn't want me to believe,

And so, he gaslights me

Into believing that his lies are true—

That these roots aren't new,

That my past isn't outgrown,

Rather evident in the battle.

To add to this bloodshed,

He shoots me, "Especially when you have depression."

You see, the Enemy just pulled the trigger
To get you to consider a possibility
That your present isn't your reality, since you look the same but have grown tremendously.

This trigger point isn't something minor,
But rather major, as it will grab your attention
And make you rethink and question
Every step you've taken.

But you have a choice to make.

Let the bullet enter your heart, make space, and penetrate,

For the lies to sprout and grow as they topple the roots that once glowed.

Or rely on what God has done in your life and use His Word to refute the "truth" the Devil wants to speak into you.

Choose wisely, for the choice you make will determine your next step in life.

Just know that your trigger point may still be in the card deck, even if you refuse to fall for his lies.

Stuck

I'm a firefly in a foggy jar, trying to figure out where I am.

Through the glass, I don't see my reflection; I see darkness instead.

I wonder if that's who I've become since I've felt trapped

Inside this hole, with no more light to guide my way out of this tunnel.

I look up at the ceiling of this room.

Might as well get cozy, considering I might not leave anytime soon.

The fact that I've been here for six months

Wasting my time reminiscing on better days with God.

"Where's your faith? Where's the courage that you'll be free?"

Well, reach inside my heart and let me know what you see.

Aren't I supposed to be the light on a hill,

Whose faith shines brighter than any star?

Who encourages others even when they feel afar

And on the verge of giving up?

Wasn't I the one to urge others to keep breathing even when they felt stuck?

Yeah, I could say that was me.

But truly, it was the Holy Spirit who spoke through me.

I'm at the end of my rope,

And I know losing faith in God is not going to help me cope

With the reality of being in a constant cycle

Of faking my emotions like I'm on display or on America's Got Talent.

I'm fighting spiritual warfare like using an umbrella against a tsunami,

While mental health tries to scare me and tear me up to make me a zombie—

Since believing that I'm still in the same place leaves me on autopilot—

There's no way I could perform CPR on my body

And get my light to shine again.

Or am I wrong?

Perhaps someone could clean up my glass,

Get the speck out of my eye, and give me a new lens

That hope isn't gone yet.

But what am I left to believe when I've been in the same place for so long?

Faith Crisis

It all started with turmoil—

Not really surprised, because I've been down this road before—

Thinking about all the possibilities of how this could be different from the other things—

The other cycles that had come previously,

The ones that left me horrendously deceived—

But this was something different.

It was a threat, an attack, a heresy—

The belief that God didn't save me.

Who would undoubtedly believe that?

Well, unfortunately, I did.

It left me tremendously confused.

At the time, I already had things on my plate—

Assignments to turn in—make sure they're not late.

I hit the snooze button on all the grief, all the mistakes, and the warning signs, not believing they would come back to me—

But as you can tell, they did eventually.

I hid them under the facade and the makeup of my mask:

That one Christian who keeps God first, not last—

One who reads and prays every day—

"She's such an example," much more they would say.

But truthfully, I'm not all that they see in me.

I'm a girl who struggles and overthinks.

One who feels bound by the shackles of her past,

With the devil taunting her to believe that her faith wouldn't last.

For the tongue can bring life and death, and the right prompt can enable my lips to move, so this must've been what the devil has been so encouraged to do:

"Make sure that she doesn't believe again.

Crush her faith; don't let her think of her sin.

Let the pain emerge from within,

Highlighting what God failed to do—

Bandage her deepest wounds,

And leave her defenseless to infections...

Man, she must have no clue

What we have in store for her:

Abandoned, apocalyptic affliction.

She can wear the facade; make sure it becomes her new skin.

If it gets itchy, throw a distraction in the way—

Most likely homework—which makes her stay up late,

Or a mental health question that makes her head ache.

Whatever it is, we need to make sure she'll never believe that she would be whoever God intended for herself to be."

I adjusted quickly but never felt comfortable.

I was assigned to the passenger seat of my life, as if I was sitting in a convertible.

Not even sure when I transitioned from being the pilot,

For where I was going was no longer recognizable.

Part of me was trying to remain conscious to not fall into the darkness,

Which felt satisfying as I sank into my seat.

But another part of me was tired of fighting and wanted to give in to the anesthesia—

The coma that would follow, leaving me mistaking darkness for light as if I were in euphoria.

Christians are supposed to resist the Devil,

But what do you do when you're exhausted and agonized by his multitude of bees—

Sent to sting your heart with lies that warp your intended design?

I'm sitting in the classroom, completing these assignments with this in my mind;

On one side, I hear God asking me to open up and confide in Him—

Like I do all the time.

But I'm not sure He knows that my mustard tree's roots have been shaky since

I started questioning exactly what and where the roots of my faith tree had been planted.

On the other side, it's quieter;

I'm just glaring at my friends as if I'm watching them through a monitor—

Not sure what my next step is, since I've been following the bell schedule instead of living out my actual presence…

Until May 17, 2023, she broke the facade.

A new breath of fresh air filled her lungs as she started the waterfall—

One that was so delayed;

Hoping that her dilemmas flowed through it all,

Her transparency would hopefully soften the fall.

Soften the clay mold she made around her heart, one that wasn't guarded as well as she thought.

One that apparently needed to come down, like the mask that used to hide the creases of her frowns.

She believed she was alone and that no one would understand anything or what she'd gone through:

Minutes of unbearable weeping, but no tears to show for the pain.

Thoughts that left scars, as they were made in vain.

Images that displayed the worst, as if she was still insane.

But only one thing was on her mind through her pain: her faith.

What is it placed on?

The past or the future?

She pondered these as the waterfall continued, until it stopped at a foggy, shimmering spring.

Her friends comforted her and reminded her that she was not alone;

That she could talk to them at any time.

And disregarding their inexperience or unrelatability, they'd always be by her side—

There for the worst and best parts of her,

Which wasn't something she thought she could believe.

She blamed herself for the loss of her former friendships;

Claiming that talking about her problems too much was why they left.

However, the audience had another point of view in mind.

They believed that real friends would stay with you through the night—

Through the storm, not just the sunny days;

Through the vacant, when you forget to pray;

Through the triumph, when you've been given grace;

Through the distant, quiet facade.

The best piece of advice she'd received collectively was about what God would do—

God will never leave you.

He's got you, no need to worry about strength.

You just got to trust that He'll lift you up from this grave—

Through this moment where you're buried deep inside your thoughts,

When all you see at the end of the tunnel is darkness nonstop—

They proclaimed that God will win this battle, even though she felt that she lost—

That God was still in control, even though I was not.

That God is with me through the autopilot moments.

Distancing myself from others doesn't mean that God will stay silent.

He will not leave me in torment.

She was grateful, as she stored these messages within her heart.

With the mask dismantled, she learned she could breathe again.

Lifesaver

Healing

It's hard—
It's hard coming to You in prayer
With scars—
The scabs I didn't want You to see
Or really,
I didn't know I had in me.

I'm coming back from a fight,
And here I am trying to pray tonight,
While battling the crowd telling me:
"I'm alone, there's no grace, no hope—
Just bondage, just chains, just condemnation."
That remains, or that's been washed up
From the sea after trying to keep my nose above the
water,
Enough to at least breathe
And feel the sun
That has yet to shine
Again in this walk.

"You are loved more than you know,

And that will never change, despite whether your scars are shown.

This season is a chance to grow.

Don't forget that I am proud of you as my love for you overflows,

My child."

—God

Set Free

Dear God,

The shackles of my past make me feel lost,
Mistaking the path I'm on,
Unaware of which direction I'm moving—
My past? My future? Which path am I choosing?

I don't know what it's like to be in the process of being set free.
And when I am, will I miss the joy that comes in between?
The trial that I endured for my perseverance—
Where am I on this path of redemption?

"Kezia, you've been redeemed from sin.
Your faith has made you right with me.
You've been set free— for you're a new creation.
However, your flesh desires the satisfaction of sin.
As you continue to resist, your faith strengthens.
That's why you have to keep fighting, my friend.
The fight is not over."
—God

Gratitude

Nothing compares to Your faithfulness,
And God, I thank You.
Every time I pray, I know You're there.
Even when I falter, You've never forsaken me.

I don't deserve that.
I've sinned too much,
But not enough
To cancel out Your love.

Not enough for You
To stop seeking me
And reminding me of Your promises,
Your teachings, Your words.
And for that, I thank You.

There's something shining bright: Your love
And faithfulness.
The two things I can look forward to.
Thank You for not giving up on me.
And always raising me up

On my lowest days, talking with me on my quietest
days,

And reaching out when I needed it the most.

Honestly, Your timing is on key.

I thank You for what it has brought me:

Gratitude for Your love,

Peace, and faithfulness—

Which You should've shown to me.

I don't think I can fully grasp Your love,

For it is something that exceeds my cup,

Dripping down and even overflowing

Into the lives of those around me.

In every season, I come to acknowledge

How it never ends—Your love, Your grace, Your
forgiveness.

There's truly no one like You.

Relief

I was back in this spot again,
With my relationship with God not at its best.
I was wasting time, indulging in distractions.

I never actually felt peace
Until I got on my knees
And cast my cares on God.
I felt more relieved
As they rolled off my tongue,
With great lengths into how my feelings were
And now, what it was—
Relief.
I relearned a valuable lesson:
Cast your cares on God,
Even when it's hard,
Because He loves you too much
To leave you with painful scars.

Dear Younger Me

Things that He Went Through

It's interesting to think about the things that He went through

to offer us a chance at eternal life and a restored relationship with God.

We don't even deserve it because of the things we've done;

All our selfish ambitions make this true.

We simply sin every day,

And we don't think about what God did.

We don't think about the result of our sin.

You see, we are supposed to turn away from sin

And stay far away.

But some become lukewarm,

Feeling natural with sinning every day.

The darkness of sin

Can change who you are.

We need to stay clean from within

And repent from what made us stray so far.

But that's not just who sinners are.

We don't deserve Him,

But His grace has reached this far.

We see people praising Him.

Just look around and hear.

They sing all kinds of hymns and songs that reach our ears.

But does it actually reach their hearts?

Some don't understand what He truly did,

And that's why I'm going to explain it to you:

He was betrayed by Judas

Who handed Him over to the Pharisees.

Died on the cross for you and me,

So that we may have a restored relationship with God

And eternal life.

Therefore, putting death to shame

And giving us a new name,

If we believe that Jesus was God's Son

And He rose three days later from the grave,

Then we become saved—

Not by the good works we do.

But by putting our faith in Him and by God's grace—

Can we say amen, for God has given us grace?

God bless y'all.

Ephesians 1

God decided to make us His own children through Jesus Christ,

And in Christ, we were made free by His blood sacrifice.

You see, it's not by our works or what we do right,

But by God's Grace through Faith in His Son, Jesus Christ.

Therefore, we can be thankful for the kindness He has lavished on us.

Even before we were created, He still gave us His love.

A blessing—to be called His daughters and sons—

And in it, we've been chosen ever since time begun.

Acknowledging our sin and iniquities,

God sent His Son to set us free.

And by His blood, we have been redeemed—

Just ONE of God's plans that did proceed.

When we hear the Good News and believe in Christ—

Changing our hearts and lives—and, in the name of Jesus Christ, to be baptized,

We get the Holy Spirit, which is God's special, promised mark on us.

Through it, we are given what God has guaranteed,

And soon, we will be set free.

Then the Lord, our God, will have praise and glory.

My Story

When I was younger,
I wasn't who I claimed to be.
Now, reflecting back, I see
The change

That occurred in my lifestyle
After giving my life
To Jesus Christ.

Ever since that day,
I became more passionate about prayer,
More determined to produce
The fruits of the Spirit and learn the Truth.

Before then, being a Christian wasn't my main focus;
Instead, it was the world that left me broken,
Fulfilling my temporary desires
That I thought would last more than an hour.

But now I see that I was greatly deceived,
Thinking that the things of this world would satisfy
me—

Being in a romantic relationship, popularity, and wealth.

Eventually, you get to the point where you will not always be yourself.

You will be wanting more, not realizing that you're opening up the door

To try to see which puzzle piece would fill your heart.

You'll come to realize that only Jesus can,

And it's been like that from the start.

These worldly products will not get you far;

Instead, they are poisons that will leave you distraught,

Intoxicating your heart with the belief that they are nutritious

While they slowly choke and cut off circulation

As you indulge in their "deliciousness."

Convinced of your pleasure within their product,

They offer and offer, hoping that you will not realize you're allergic,

For their "benefits" leave you distracted, as they are stealing money out of your pocket.

Bittersweet.

Not many realize it.

How worldly things distract you from your heart's

condition, and you don't see it until you realize the Truth.

That's why I am telling you:

Jesus set me free

From all of this deception.

He's my Rock and Foundation,

And He is also King.

I remember that day I gave my life to Christ;

My depression went away that night,

Joy overflowed in my heart.

I never felt more free from the shackles that chained me in the dark.

Real Love

I know you once dreamed of a fairytale romance,

Wanting a spouse who would love you till the very end—

One who would choose you instead of your best friend,

One who could love you to a high extent,

One who actually stays and chooses to listen.

You hoped he would fulfill you like no one else can,

As you assumed, that is where real love comes from.

But instead, real love comes from a man who chose to take your place at the cross,

Who knew all of your flaws and still found you worthy of His love—

A love that exceeds the limitations of measurement.

For it is unlimited and shared upon many generations.

So how is real love defined?

In Christ.

The One who died for His friends

When we deserved to perish,

The One who is humble in heart,

And meek in spirit,

The One who keeps His promises

And walks in forgiveness,

The One who is not quickly enraged,

But swift with perseverance,

The One who obeys His Father

And delights in His will, which is perfect,

The One who rejoices with the truth

And not in wickedness.

Little did you know He is THE EVERLASTING LOVE you were looking for,

Which couldn't originate in man, but in Christ evermore.

Don't get me wrong—

Romantic love can be nice,

But it cannot be compared to the love of Christ.

You don't need a guy to tell you that you're worth it

When Christ proved that by His actions.

You don't need a guy to convince you that you're beautiful

When Yahweh declared you're fearfully and wonderfully made, you're perfect.

You don't need a guy to establish what real love is

When Jesus defined it by His blood.

Late Night Talk Show

I remember where it all started.

One night in my room,

I prayed that He would rescue me

And save me from the tide,

From the waves I had been submerged under for so long—all my life.

Hoping that one more night I might survive,

Enough to glance at the moon, a light—a desire inside—

To finally feel satisfied.

To finally feel enough.

To finally feel heard.

To finally feel free.

Suddenly, the current grew weaker.

As I gathered my last attempt to stay afloat,

There it was—a dim sign:

"Starring Tonight: Talking with God."

Not even two steps in, we locked eyes.

He wasn't even surprised.

He welcomed me into His arms and

Smiled with me while I tore myself apart.

Before I knew it, I was surrounded by His embrace, His empathy.

My eyes were closed, yet I still felt His warmth penetrate through the wet clothes I had on me.

We hugged for what felt like a lifetime as I confessed my disgrace,

Broke down my burdens, insecurities, and my fears,

Knowing that He was right here.

And as I continued,

I sensed His smile—

The "My Child has come home."

The "This is My Daughter."

And I just have never been loved like this before.

The best part was—He never let me go.

He stayed, listened, and comforted.

No wonder I never felt fulfilled.

Not knowing that Jesus is love,

The light I was looking for,

Like the moon

Guiding me through the night and even my blues.

There to wipe my tears.

There to hold my hand.

There to say I got to get back up when I couldn't stand.

And little did I know that this was not the end,

But rather the beginning,

As I would meet with Him every hour,

Laughing, confessing, crying—whatever the status quo—

As if it was on live television, with no drama though.

Being honest with the King,

Talking with God, the Host,

One-on-one, this time, as a disciple.

No cameras,

No lights,

No makeup,

Just you and your Father,

Or rather, Best Friend,

As you discuss many topics

In the lounge of your bed,

Sitting up and listening to every word said,

Every comment and thought.

'Starring Tonight: Talking with God'

It's much more freeing than you thought.
Being in the presence of the True King,
Nothing to hide, just you and Him—
The One who you could finally confide in.

Part Two

Season Finale

Sleep

I desire to sleep.

I desire to dream,

To get away from thoughts

And those things that

Can be distracting

From what my focus should be on—

My relationship with God.

These past days, I haven't been faithful.

I know that I am truly grateful

For the grace and love that overflows from Him—

Who is faithful,

Unlike me—

Who has been struggling

In what unfortunately resulted in

A cycle of unwanted sin.

I just wanted to get the day over with and dream—

Sleep and not think about previous actions, regrets, or behaviors.

I wanted to sleep as if my day ended better

Than how it previously was.

I learned that it's better to tell God

Than to hold onto these feelings

That will eventually impact you and be shown

And could eventually grow.

Casting your cares on God is important, from day to day.

Instead of holding on to those feelings—let them go.

Trust me, it's better to let them go than to hold on to them,

Gripping them like bones.

Break that sinful foundation—

The same foundation you should not trust or seek refuge in.

Seek God, I repeat, seek God.

I know it can be hard, but it's far better to give these things to God now

Rather than eventually waiting till time passes by.

Let these angers, confusions go.

Forgive yourself and show

The true fruits that you have produced

In your spiritual life and salvation.

Let them be shown.

Declare God faithful.

Declare yourself forgiven.

And go to sleep.

Sleep better than you would holding on to those things.

Sleep and dream.

God bless ye.

Burdens

Lowkey, I was holding on to my burdens, which left me
more broken.

Lacking self-confidence

And the ability to let go

Of what was holding me down,

As discouragement was shown.

I should let go and let God,

Literally, as referenced in *Sleep*,

Because we're supposed to cast our cares on Him,

As it says in 1 Peter 5:7, later you'll see.

The burdens have been lifted.

Things will be taken care of.

Trusting God as the day goes on,

Not worrying because God is in control,

And much more.

It may be stressful—

Whatever the burden may be—

But God is greater

Than anything.

And with God, anything is possible.

As I saw the verse of the day,

Which was Psalm 68:19,

I was moved by the word "burden,"

Which weighed heavily on me.

The weight that seems unmovable is impossible to get rid of

Until it meets God.

He cares for us; therefore, cast your burdens on Him,

I encourage you to go to God

With whatever your burdens may be,

And remember that He is able to do anything.

He is God.

The Only One Man

Same sin, but it feels different
Condemnation, intention, and the chains holding me
down.
The time to repent and what I have seen—
There's a major life change in me.

It started when He went on the cross,
Took our place because of our sin punishment,
Which results in death.
Therefore, He went on the cross, paying our debt.

I hope you know about
The Only One Man—
Who died on the cross for you
To give you a chance

For a relationship with God and eternal life,
If you choose to believe
In Him and His sacrifice.

Confessing with your mouth
And believing in your heart

That Jesus is Lord and that God raised
Him from the dead is what gets you saved.
It's not by works—
Works are a byproduct of faith.

He loves you so much
To take your place.
In Him, please place your faith.

I think it would be best
If you could learn
And have a relationship
With the One who calls your worth.

His name is Jesus Christ,
And yes, He saved my life.
He can save yours too—
Just believe, tell others about Him, and trust in Him.

Discontinue your willingness to sin.
Remember His promises and what He has said.
He loves you so much more—more than anything
Or anyone could. Nothing can compare to Him who
died on the cross.

The Only One Man is available to anyone who calls out
to Him,

And they will be saved.

Keep seeking, keep praying, keep fighting,

For your reward will be in heaven one day.

Prayer

The communication with God,
Our Savior, with whom we can share our thoughts,
Pray for others and ourselves.

Remember not to think highly of ourselves,
Don't be prideful or self-seeking
Because that isn't fulfilling what love is—
its characteristics.

The communication between us and God—
No limits, no timer, just concentration
On building and talking to the One
Who saved us by sending His Son.

Jesus Christ took our place
On the cross where He laid,
Crucified for you and me,
So our sin price would be paid.

Did you know that Jesus wants to get to know you?
A relationship is available with Truth,

Whom you can confide in and talk to
About anything and at any time.

Remember, prayer is not merely asking God for things,
Not praising God only in the valleys
But also the hills, where our faith is still growing.
Like yeast rising for a baked dough,
It takes time.

Therefore, in the valleys, keep fighting condemnation
And those things that seem to be tempting you.
The fight is ongoing—
Don't give up.

We must deny ourselves daily
And not conform to the flesh.
Prayer is more than just asking for things from Him;
It's communication with Our Savior

Who saved and saves us from the ravines of sin
Continually, as we go and confide in Him.

Psalm 32

Blessed is the one whose sins are forgiven,
And whose sin God doesn't count against them
doesn't matter what you've done, my friend
Give your guilt to God
Acknowledge your sin

Don't be silent about it
Confess it and give it to Him
He is our refuge and our hiding place
It's important to seek His face

Pray without ceasing
As it says in 1 Thessalonians 5:17
Be persistent in prayer
As it says in Luke 18:1
Never stop praying
To God's Only Son

Confessing our sin, results in forgiveness not judgment
While holding it in produces
Guilt and damage

Pray while God may be found
Don't let the mighty waters get you
Remember Luke 18:1 as well
Seek God, our refuge;

He'll instruct us in the way we should go,
And counsel us with his loving eye
Seek understanding unlike
The horse or the mule

Whom are controlled by bit and bridle
Reflect yourself In Jesus's Light.

There are many wicked deeds done
but the Lord's unfailing love
Surrounds the one
who trusts in Him

Remember, good abides in Jesus's ways-
Be the Light of the World.

Our Lord, Our God
He has many promises.
Defined in His mercy, love, and grace

Just remember to

Turn away from your ways
And take refuge in God's unfailing grace and love
It's crucial to seek His face
While He May be found

Remember to confess your sin
Acknowledging it and repenting from it
When you do that, the guilt would be forgiven
Which may had laid heavily upon your chest

He will instruct us and teach us the way we should go
Don't be silent about your sin
Confess it and give it to Him.

Rerouting

Sometimes, I get confused.

I don't know what to do.

Should I yield? Should I cruise?

Or do I keep following what the GPS is telling me to do?

I don't know,

So I follow the GPS instructions

To this place that I haven't known—but I guess remained hidden

Until later, when it's shown.

Moving forward, there's smooth sailing.

I heard the GPS tell me to take a right, but I was incorrect.

Rerouting me to my new direction, I pondered, "How could I have misheard?"

I looked up, and the GPS updated.

It told me to take a right, then a left, and then wait.

While waiting, I think of the possible directions.

The GPS in front of me told that person to go straight.

But when I did, I missed the exit.

Even though I didn't understand, the GPS rerouted me back to a soon discovery

Of a place where I was soon to be and learn new things.

This time, I paid attention.

Five minutes passed, and I'm still in the right direction.

It told me to take a right in about three minutes. I'm so thankful I'm listening to its correction,

Of telling me where to go, and now I see the beauty the path is taking me.

But then this happened:

I saw a roundabout coming up.

I didn't know what to do—I felt stuck.

I looked up and saw that the GPS told me to go straight—

Right through it, like it was a piece of cake.

Which it was, but I didn't yet see

How easier it would be

To fight knowing that the King of kings

Already won the victory.

I took two U-turns and I'm back at the roundabout.

Focused on where I'm supposed to go now,

I've now gotten a deeper meaning: I'm continually learning.

Thankful for the victory

And the direction.

For now, I see how the Rod of Correction has placed me and helped me

Get to where I need to be

In this trail, in this season,

With feelings of contentment

Of where it has directed me.

The GPS represented God

In the story,

Leading us to our destination,

For His Glory.

I rate Him 5/5 stars

For His patience and redirection,

And for rerouting us when we make every wrong turn or decision.

He is always there, helping us

Get to where we need to be.

So I hope you understand this with new meanings:

God is willing to direct you

And correct you. Please let Him in, and He will show you

Where you need to go and be.

Then, see that the end result is way better than you dreamed.

Past

Revisiting your past isn't the same as living in it.

Just like living in the past doesn't mean you're living in the present.

There's no harm in glancing over your shoulder and admiring the journey you've ventured on,

but there is harm in wanting to stay in the past and acting like you belong.

Putting back on the facade that everything is okay,

Which sooner or later, you'll learn that this would delay

the blessings you would have received

if you had just decided to take a leap of faith

and drift into a safer place.

One that doesn't chain you to your past self,

But one that branches off from refreshing roots,

To lively paths and better mental health.

One that doesn't leave you in despair and broken nights, but offers hope,

a new light, found in Jesus Christ.

There comes a time when you have to move on and choose:

either be free from the shackles or remain in them,

as they become more comfortable while the pain clenches and numbs your skin.

Before you make a decision, consider how much you've grown.

Never forget that you are a better person than the mirror reflection of your past shows.

Every single day that you're breathing is a baby step in the right direction of healing.

On the roughest days, I encourage you to continue walking,

even if it is an increment as small as a grain of sand.

Know that, in the end, you will continue to grow if you start to move.

Eventually, you'll see how your baby steps have transformed into your unique footprint.

When you glance back, considering the meltdowns and triumphs you've experienced on the way,

you will be proud that you never strayed.

There's an angelic aroma within reflection, but shackles within being stagnant,

because revisiting your past isn't the same as living in it.

Kezia Kyei-Boahen

License of Change

God's grace is not meant to be used as a license to continue sinning,

But rather, an opportunity to change from your fleshly dwelling.

While it is hard to fight your inner desires, we must not forsake the grace

By which we have never acquired by our own merit for our sins erased.

With this, I urge you to exchange your license of sin for a license of change,

For the sacrifice made on the cross was not in vain.

It was not made so that we can continue sinning,

But rather to run back to our Father as we start our new beginning.

Through the depths of our trials,

The sunrises of our triumphs,

There's more to this life than living in assimilation to our sin.

We must repent and return to the new life that began with His resurrection.

Refresh & Fight

It's hard coming back to Christ
When you know you've sinned.
The enemy tries to get in your head—
Don't listen to him.

Telling you lies,
Letting sin be normalized,
Filling your mind with negativity,
Which makes it hard to see
The light; the hope that is shining within me.

Shame, guilt, and condemnation
Prevent the consistency of my prayer life
When those words are repeated in my mind.

Don't be afraid of what God's going to say,
But be reminded of His grace.
He casts our sin as far as the east is from the west.
He won't put you to the test,
But through your trials, come back to Him.
He can redeem you once again.

Remember He loves you.

His blood was shed on the cross for that.

Even when you sin, you can still come back.

Be transparent with Him and pray about your struggles.

He can aid you when you have trouble.

Let God's words flow through your mind

As you fight the devil's lies.

Repeat Scripture daily,

Speak truth into your life,

As Heaven cheers you on from the sidelines.

Don't give the devil a foothold,

Rebuke him before he tries

To knock you down one more time.

Remember to fight with the armor that God provides.

There's grace for your sin

That comes from Him—

Whose blood was shed

For the transgressions of men.

So remember, there is grace that abides in He

Who loves you without question.

Don't use this as a license to sin,

Use it as a way to get back on track to Him.

Remember to feed your spirit and starve your flesh,

Show the same grace to others as you've received from Him.

Don't give in to the devil's tactics and lies,

But remember not to give up the fight.

The Surgery

Looking down at the new stitches that surface the horizon of your skin,

Wondering what blood, sweat, and tears had lied beneath and within.

The overgrown roots that needed to be taken care of

Yet continued to bruise as if you were unaware of

Its presence.

Its essence,

The scars that remind you of your pain,

Or rather, the experience of how you got hurt in the first place.

And at times, you fear that the stitches may become undone.

Instead, your scars are the remnants of who you once were.

The pain you go through is necessary,

For you to reflect and be proud of how far you've come.

As you continue to venture on your journey,

Remember to find relief in knowing that the battle has been won.

Gardening 101

In those seasons when you aren't bearing fruit

In quantity as you hoped or in great quality,

Be grateful that a fruit was produced,

And by that, you can adjust to something new.

If the fruit was good,

Work on the quantity.

Practice that Fruit of the Spirit

By abiding in Christ

So it becomes natural in the soil of your heart for it to grow.

Therefore, more of that fruit would be shown.

If the fruit was bad,

Work on the quality.

Don't condemn yourself, but gently restore and uplift yourself to grow something different

In the soil of your heart.

Don't forget to be patient, and remember that it takes time.

If there is no fruit,

Think about the seeds.

Which seeds do you want to be there, and how can you work on practicing it?

Ask your neighbor

Which fruits they see,

And reflect and adjust based on that.

The fruits in your heart are very important.

They can start to grow and fill up the whole space of your heart.

Make sure it's the right fruit you would like the Farmer to see.

Phototropism

The choices you make inspire the direction of your life,
leading to walking in darkness or in light.

If you walk in light,
You should demonstrate your embracement of the
Gospel,
As you highlight the contrast from dark to light
And continue to see the change in your life.

This contrast is abundant
In a way that someone can see your life and
Inspired to be changed and become saved
From the darkness that lurks around them every day,
The temptations that can lead them astray,
As they've been deceived about what is light—

Light isn't distractions or things that seem right—
It's alive, it's Jesus, it's love, it's being kind—
The characteristics you should soon represent
As light fills you from your feet to your head.

Shining like a lighthouse to the darkness that resides

In other people's lives, to open up their eyes

To see, there's an option of light inside

That is contrasted to the darkness that resides.

The seed of the Gospel can fully be rooted in the soil of your hearts.

Please believe and try not to depart

From the messages that were preached and shared from the start,

In order to know what it means to have a light-filling heart.

Reminders

Scripture says that we should "walk by faith and not by sight."
It says it in Second Corinthians, chapter five, verse seven.

I should be reflecting on my day each night,
Seeing what I did wrong, noticing what I did right,
And reminding myself of Jesus's light.

Lately, I've been having a hard time
Walking by faith and not by sight,
Especially when I rely on my feelings,
Which can be a bit deceiving.

This later has an impact on my actions,
Leading to devastating dissatisfaction.
Instead, I should remember and be renewed
By the promises of Jesus
Rather than my feelings each time.

I can pray anywhere, at any time,
And let Jesus's promises be fresh upon my mind.

I look to Him because He is rich in mercy,

And I should be in the Word daily.

I remind myself of my identity in Christ—

Being God's child, His sheep, and His creation,

Being renewed and redeemed from sin, as well as condemnation.

By His grace and love, I'm saved through faith,

And He is mighty to guide me as my Shepherd.

I should also walk in the Spirit

And pray to hate what God hates—sin,

And pray to love who God loves—His creation.

I remind myself not to trust in the lies of the devil

And not to give up when I have struggles.

I go to my Savior, who wants to aid me and hear my troubles.

I have to remember I can pray about anything, anytime, and anywhere,

And to "walk by faith and not by sight"—

As it says in Second Corinthians. chapter five, verse seven.

Restore

Do you ever feel knocked down?
Like you don't know the way out?
This cycle of self-pity and self-doubt
Keeps taking your joy away now.

At first, you were confused,
Now you stay firm in Truth,
Knowing your identification in Him
Who saved you from depths of sin.

Sometimes, I feel overwhelmed,
Like I'm drowning in the deep end,
Waters that seem so steep,
With waves crashing over me, filled with
Lies, guilt, and opinions from the enemy,
Tempting me to think all sorts of things.

Reminding me constantly of the actions I've made,
The steps I take,
The path I've chosen,
And confusing different pathways

That aren't narrow or even straight,
That don't align with God's Word,
That aren't a piece of cake.

In order to prevent me from my purpose,
In order to start a diversion,
Persuading me of no purpose,
Taking me into deep oceans,

To drown me in the lies,
Of hate and disguise.
But then, not in surprise,
I see God, the Light.

Creating a way out of darkness,
And giving me the armor to fight.
Putting on the breastplate of righteousness,
I know I'll be alright.

With God right beside me,
I know He's on my side.
Time to put on the armor
And start to fight.

Jeremiah 29:11 claims I have a purpose,

So I know that the devil's lies are fake.

I have a motive

To live for Christ, proclaiming the Gospel,

And being bold in my faith. The enemy is surprised, I know it.

Rebuking the devil's lies with scripture is key,

As well as praying daily.

You've got to feed your spirit with God's truth,

And as a result, you realize that when the enemy tries to knock you down, you won't move.

Gotta stay strong in faith,

Knowing that God saves,

And see how the cycle's motion ends with

New foundations in place.

Relying on God and His words,

And a change from

Self-pity to confidence,

And self-doubt to trust,

And giving glory, thanks, and honor to the one we must—God..

Recap

On the days when my relationship with God isn't the best,

My recap leaves me in distress.

Feeling far from God and falling short once again,

Especially slipping back into cycles of sin.

Breaking a scab that had just healed,

Leading to my sorrow in this hole that's been dug deeper—

The sin cycle.

The sin, which causes death,

Leaves me stressed as I am tempted, worrying about what's next—

Will it get better?

Will I become faithful again?

Will I overcome this hurdle of sin?

Fight against it and win the race,

By getting back up and not letting it take my place—

In feeling stuck because I know God is with me.

In the depths of devastation and victory,

He is rooting for me and encouraging me

To keep going.

I appreciate Him for that.

He never gave up on me.

Therefore, I shouldn't either.

Recaps can lead to heartfelt feelings—

Excitement, disappointment, or something else.

But one thing to remember

Is God's involvement

In your life and what He does:

Bringing peace, joy, and satisfaction,

Knowing that He is your best friend,

The only one who can fully comprehend everything in my head—

And is still rooting for me no matter what.

Hope

Hold your head up high, even when it feels like clouds are falling from the sky.

When the air is moist and the puddles are becoming deeper, keep your head up and breathe.

You know that eventually, it will get better because of God's will for you.

Gotta have a positive attitude.

Even though it may be hard right now, it doesn't mean it will remain that way

Have hope and pray.

Don't give up.

Don't lose faith.

In The Current

Intermission

You know that joy that comes in the morning?
After the trials, all the hard work, and all of the mourning,
After all the trusting in God and focusing on Him—

You see how the hard work paid off when you don't conform to sin?

Yeah, I know it's amazing.
It's unfathomable when you're in the dirt,
When you don't feel like getting up,
When you're on the edge of losing faith,
When you feel nothing but stuck.
But then you remember: God never gave up.

He has good plans for you—
To prosper and not to harm you.
So, in His promises, trust, and you'll see you got here—
Not by luck, but by blessings, by perseverance, and most importantly, by faith!

The hard part is remembering the things you've learned

And putting them to use in the good work that God has started in you.

To bear more fruit, connect to the vine and to truth, while knowing that God is with you!

In your transition period,

Where the days are getting less joyful

And the windshield is becoming blurry,

Remember to look back on the mission

And stay connected to what you've learned to move forward in the journey when you're in intermission.

Raindrops

It took me a while to notice this,

But I hope I remember it:

The small little things count,

Like raindrops that go from the sky to the ground;

They travel through all of their cycles to find their way back to the cloud.

In many ways, this is a metaphor,

And in some, it's a story.

In trials, in tribulations,

I put in my best work—

The best I can do without burning out.

And I realized that what I do then impacts my current state.

If I hadn't persevered, then only God knows where I'd be instead.

For the little things count;

A lot of people say 'time is money,' but without these—

The prayers, the 12 am Bible studies, the early morning devotions—

I would still have hesitation. The taunting, the
judgment, and the misconceptions

That originate from temptations would have rerouted
my destination.

Raindrops add up like puddles,

And puddles become streams,

And streams can flow to become a river,

And eventually a lake so that

Raindrops can become oceans,

Like how grains of sand can become a beach.

So imagine your faith if you continued to believe.

Faith is one of the most valuable currencies.

Wisdom is also one of them. With both, imagine your
life—

Believing while growing, thus allowing you to thrive

As you know the differences between wrong and right.

Therefore, our little actions add up,

Like a couple of raindrops that were once alone,

Starting to group up

Until they become one.

Raindrops are tiny on their own,

But together, they can be as big as a puddle or an ocean. The small things count.

Our Hero

Every day, we have a new page added to our story—
Our book, our life, all for His glory,
Which includes details about His sacrifice,
And how willingly He offered to give His life—

For a chance for us to be saved
And to know about His grace,
Which we are fulfilled by each day,
As He saves us from the attacks of the enemy,
And guides us as we become saved.

Later, we can pour out what He's poured in—
The never-ending fountain of His love vs. our sin.
How willing He is to serve others and for us to be His friends,
As we pray and He forgives us all over again.

As we do this, we remind the generations who have and are to come
About the characteristics of God's only begotten Son,
Who has been faithful to us and His Father,

As we are His ambassadors and have become His sons and daughters.

To those who are struggling from within,

I want you to know that there is a hero—

The only One Man who came to save you,

And I want to remind you that the devil has won zero.

Psalm 46

Never forget who God is.

He created the world,

Which was formed from His lips;

The One who freed the Israelites from the Egyptians,

And most importantly, the One who sent His Son to die for our sins.

God is greater than our troubles, our nations, and our armor.

When mountains tremble and the earth shakes,

We will not be afraid

Because we know His name.

I want you to know that He is a safe place,

One that you can go to when your head aches,

One you can confide in because of His embrace,

And One you can trust since He is our strength.

God is our safety and refuge,

One who doesn't change, unlike an eroded statue.

Remember that He is our God, our faithful hand,

And that we shall never forget who He is, even in the end.

Influence

*"In the same way, let your light shine before others, that
they may see your good deeds and glorify your Father in
heaven."*
— Matthew 5:16 NIV

Our influence matters,

Especially to those whose salvation is dire.

Our actions, by walking in truth, can produce

Questions about Jesus—

The One we should be like—

Walking in steps that are like Christ's

To impact the lives

Of those who don't know about His sacrifice.

Or perhaps they do,

But they don't realize

The power influence

Has on their lives.

If we walk by faith and align ourselves with Christ,

More people can be saved

And know about His sacrifice.

With questions being raised about who He is
And our identification in Him,
It can increase their desire
To find worth in Christ rather than in worldly lifestyles.

But if we align ourselves with worldly expectations
Of what we are supposed to be like,
Then we get separated
From how we're supposed to be like in Christ.

We can't follow the world and follow Christ.
They support two different lives—
One that abides in sin, which is normalized,
And one that abides in Him and His sacrifice.

In addition to this, influence has a role in the choices we
make in our daily lives,
As well as in the opinions and actions that occur in our
hearts and what they emphasize.
So be careful of your influencers because of how they
can impact your lives.

Your influence matters
Because it has the power

To inspire or bring direction
To different things.

Walking out our faith is vital,
Especially to those who are observant.
If our actions support our faith,
Then that can raise questions about His grace
And bring honor and glory to His name.

Past, Present, and Future

Can we just sit back and admire?
God's promises and what they have inspired,
And what they continue to do
As we listen to truth.

As I reflect on myself, I remember how I used to be—
Indulging in sin like every other human being.
Though I did it willingly, I hadn't yet seen
God's plan that would intervene.

I wouldn't have thought I would be here,
Writing poetry with the Holy Spirit,
With a clear objective—

To bring community to those who need it,
Or to inspire those who need encouragement,
To walk in truth through discernment
While producing the fruit of the Spirit.

God has delivered me from so much that I can't even list it.
He has healed me from what I've experienced,

Bringing new life, appreciating and understanding what it means to be in His midst,

While making Christ-like decisions as I live for Him.

I remember when I was born again,

My joy was and still is incomparable.

As I live for God, not for the desires of men (the fleshly desires),

The number of lessons I've learned are numerous.

Every season, my faith grows stronger because I learn something new,

Just like in James, chapter one, verses two and three,

It tells us that "the testing of our faith produces endurance."

With that, I can have perseverance.

Additionally, as I learn more about God,

I become more amazed

By the overwhelming fountain

Of His love and grace,

Which seems unlimited—it is—and it's amazing how all this comes from Him—

Who created the world from the beginning,

Making us all in His image,

And sending His Son, who died on the cross without blemish,

Taking our place, which we should be extremely grateful for,

To provide salvation from sin with His love overflowing even more.

I cannot truly express my gratitude for all that God has done,

But just imagine what God will do in the present based on what He has accomplished through His Son.

Towards the future, we should continue to love

Like Christ does,

Continuing to reach more generations who are to come.

Biblical References

Please note that some poems share Bible verses.

Made New

What is Home?: Romans 8:1, 1 Thessalonians 5:16

Lukewarm: Psalm 85:2, 2 Corinthians 5:17, Matthew 5:14

Unworthy: Psalms 85:2, Philippians 4:13, 1 Corinthians 10:13

Bold faith: Romans 1:16, Ephesians 4:3

The Shifting Tide

Can I be real?: Proverbs 3:5-6, Philippians 1:6, 1 Peter 5:7,

1 Peter 5:9, 2 Corinthians 5:20

Growing Plant: Revelation 3:16, James 1:2-4

Numb: Luke 18:1

Motion Sickness: Psalm 18:35

Under the Surface

Counterfeit: Proverbs 26:11

Backsliding: Exodus 17:11-13

Spiral Street: 2 Corinthians 5:17, Romans 8:1, Hebrews 4:15-16, Matthew 28:20, 2 Corinthians 12:9

Rest Stop: Romans 5:3-5

(Welcome Back)

Trigger Point: Deuteronomy 31:6, John 8:44, 1 Peter 5:8

Stuck: Matthew 5:14-16, 1 Thessalonians 5:11

Faith Crisis: Colossians 3:2, Proverbs 18:21, Proverbs 4:23

Proverbs 17:17, 2 Chronicles 20:17

Lifesaver

Healing: Psalms 34:18: John 8:36

Set Free: Galatians 5:16-17, Romans 5:1, James 1:2-4

Gratitude: 1 Corinthians 1:9, Romans 8:38-39, Romans 5:5, Psalms 36:5

Relief: 1 Peter 5:7, Psalms 55:22

Dear Younger Me

Things that He went Through: Matthew 26, Romans 5:8;6, Ephesians 2:8-9, 1 John 3:16-18

Ephesians 1: Ephesians 1:4-14; 2:8-9; Romans 5:8

John 3:16

My Story: 1 John 2:15-17, James 1:14-15, Proverbs 5:3-5

Real Love: Psalms 136:26, John 15:13, Matthew 11:29,

1 Corinthians 13:4-8

Late Night Talk Show: 1 John 4:8

Season Finale

Sleep: 2 Corinthians 5:7, Galatians 5, 1 Peter 5:7, Proverbs 28:13

Burdens: Psalm 68:19, Matthew 11:28-30, 1 Peter 5:7

The Only One Man: Matthew 5:12, Romans 6:23; 10:9-10;

Ephesians 2:8-9

Prayer: Romans 8:1; 12:2; Psalm 46

Psalm 32: Psalm 32, Isaiah 55:6-13

Rerouting: Psalms 32:8

Past: Matthew 5:14, Romans 5:8, 2 Corinthians 5:17, John 8:11, I John 1:9

License of Change: Hebrews 10:26-27, 2 Chronicles 7:14

Refresh & Fight: Psalm 103:12, Ephesians 1:7; 6:11, James 1:2-4, 2 Chronicles 7:14, James 1:2-4, Philippians 4:6-7,

Ephesians 5, Hebrews 4:16

Gardening 101: Galatians 5:19-23; John 15:4

Phototropism: Romans 8:5-6, Matthew 6:22-23

Reminders: 2 Corinthians 5:7, Romans 8:1; 12:9

Restore: Ephesians 6:10-18, Jeremiah 29:11, Mark 16:15,

2 Timothy 4:2

Recap: Romans 3:23, Hebrews 12:1, Psalm 37:49

In the Current

Intermission: Philippians 1:6, Philippians 2:12-13

Our hero: Romans 8:38-39

Psalm 46: Psalm 46

Influence: Matthew 5:16, Romans 10, 2 Corinthians 5:7; 17:20

Past, Present and Future: James 1:2-3, Psalms 139:14-15, 2 Corinthians 5:21, Ephesians 2:4-5

Acknowledgments

Jesus- Thank you for always being there when I felt alone, as the waves of my past and my current struggles tried to submerge me under condemnation. Thank you for being my lifesaver.

My Parents, Barb and Adu- Thank you for leading me to Christ, praying for me both before and after I was saved, and encouraging me to write this book.

My Brother, Ryan- Thank you for always being real with me, for all the rides to Church, and for never failing to lighten the mood with your jokes.

The Boadi Family- Thank you for guiding me in every aspect and supporting me throughout my faith journey.

Pastor Matt Gardner and **Ms. Michelle James**- Thank you for consistently being there for me and mentoring me in my faith.

Mrs. Regina Felty, Ms. Praise S, and **Ms. Anderline Cadet**- Your motivation and published work have encouraged and uplifted me in ways I cannot express. I am truly grateful for your mentorship in creating this book as well as in my relationship with God.

Lili Skinner, Liana Torres, Katherine Morales-Hernandez, Jules Gilmister, Kori Doyle, Nicole Kyei-Asare, and **Zeta Mansapit; Aaron Kyei-Asare, Alex Vargas-Nieves, Christian Ghisoiu, Jack Warrick,**

Sean McGrady, Olamide Makinde, Paa Woode, and more- Thank you for motivating me to not only keep moving forward in writing this book but also in my faith. I thank God for our iron-sharpening friendships, in which we are able to encourage, love, and laugh with each other. Thank you for being my closest friends, whom I can confide in.

I would also like to thank my close friends and family, who may not be mentioned explicitly. I am thankful for you and I love you. I appreciate how much you've reminded me to not be too hard on myself and to be able to grow and be the Christian I am today. Thank you for motivating me and reminding me to not give up! I thank God for speaking through you guys, so I can grow even closer to God.

Finally, I would like to thank you, my readers! I hope this book brings insight, encouragement, and relatability, assuring you that you are not alone and that Jesus loves you. Your support and enthusiasm have been heartfelt. Thank you for taking the time to engage with this book. May it uplift you and bring you closer to Christ. God bless :D

About the Poet

Kezia Kyei-Boahen is a poet and writer born and raised in Maryland. She discovered her love for poetry during her teenage years. Before falling in love with poetry, she created her own homemade books centered around her love and desire for a puppy when she was eight. Now, she drafts poetry inspired by her love for Jesus.

Beyond writing poetry, Kezia enjoys Bible studies, playing the ukulele and creating songs, watching *Psych*, and hanging out with her friends. She believes in using her gift of poetry to bring others closer to Christ, fostering a sense of healing and community.

You can follow Kezia's literary journey on Instagram and TikTok at @Kezia.Writes! Thank you so much for reading :D

www.ingramcontent.com/pod-product-compliance
Lightning Source LLC
Chambersburg PA
CBHW070706130626
46553CB00005B/1862